To:

_____

From:

_____

Date:

_____

Published in Nashville, Tennessee, by Thomas Nelson, Inc.
Thomas Nelson is a registered trademark of Thomas Nelson, Inc.

Published in association with Creative Trust, Inc., a literary and entertainment management company.
www.CreativeTrust.com

The Scripture quotation in this book is from *The Message* (MSG) © 1993.
Used by permission of NavPress Publishing Group.

Personal testimonies appearing in this book are used by permission of the authors.

Project Editor: Jessica Inman
Project Developer: Lisa Stilwell
Design by Koechel Peterson Design, Minneapolis, Minnesota

Photos on pages 5, 26 (Caleb Chapman and Julia), Emily (age 13) with Steven Curtis Chapman on page 30, and sillouettes on page 39 courtesy of Mary Beth Chapman
Photo on page 7 courtesy of John Price Photo / www.johnpricephoto.com
Photos of Emily (age 20) on page 30 and sheet music on page 39 courtesy of Jason Tucker / www.tuckerphotography.com
Photo on page 51 courtesy of Austin Mann
Photo on page 63 courtesy of Mark DeLong / www.delongphoto.com

ISBN-10: 1-4041-0522-0
ISBN-13: 978-1-4041-0522-5

Printed and bound in the United States

www.thomasnelson.com

Cinderella

THE LOVE OF A DADDY AND HIS PRINCESS

Steven Curtis Chapman

THOMAS NELSON
Since 1798

NASHVILLE   DALLAS   MEXICO CITY   RIO DE JANEIRO   BEIJING

Introduction

One night as I was trying to do some writing for my album *This Moment*—
"trying" being the key word in that sentence—I took on bath duty with my two
littlest girls. Stevey Joy and Maria were both three years old at the time, and they
did not at all share my concern that bath time should run efficiently. In fact, quite
the opposite: every time I turned around to get shampoo or a wash cloth, I looked
back at the tub and saw only ripples in the bathwater, no girls. Where did they go?
A few moments later I heard the giggles and saw the two princesses, Cinderella and
Snow White (with a little help from Disney costumes), cheering, "We're going to a
ball, Daddy!" I was stressed with my workload, frustrated, and tired, and it was
already late—well past an acceptable bedtime. "No," I corrected, "you're not going to
the ball, you're going in the tub."

Finally, after foiling two or three of their attempts to escape, I managed to get
them dried off and hurried them to bed. "Dad, read us a story," they pleaded. "No, no
stories tonight! It's too late," I said. "We're going to pray, pray quick, and go to bed!
Pray a short prayer, immediate family only! Just pray, fast." I was so frustrated. I had
to go back to work—I was trying to write these songs and make some progress on
the album. And finally, I got them to bed. "No, no more drinks of water! Nothing!
Go to sleep! I love you. Good night. Lights off. Kisses. Good night."

I closed the door, and it hit me. I felt as if God leaned down and whispered this name: Emily Chapman. And I knew immediately that He was speaking to my heart. You see, my daughter Emily is now twenty-one years old, and she's grown and gone off and is changing the world herself. And God was saying to me, "Steven, you big knucklehead, are you really going to rush through these moments like this and miss these priceless snapshots in time? Because you know how fast they'll go by. Remember little Emily?"

My wife and I have had the luxury of seeing our kids grow into wonderful young adults—and seeing with our own eyes how quickly these times really do go by. Thinking about this was very convicting and I thought, *You know what? I do this so much. I do a lot of rushing through the moment that I'm in, and I miss some important times. And I think I'm probably not alone in this. I have to write a song about these priceless moments so that I won't forget, and maybe I can help someone else remember it too.*

That's the story behind the song "Cinderella" and the book you hold in your hands.

Maria and Stevey Joy

I worry about the five minutes or five days or five years ahead. Or I look over my shoulder and say, "Boy, that was great back there," or "I should have done this back there." God's really been teaching me about making sure I'm showing up in the moment He's placed me in—the good ones, the hard ones, the happy ones, the sad ones—every single moment. The moments on stage with my sons as the proudest dad on the planet, thanking God for this gift of getting to tour with Caleb and Will in my band, as well as that moment at 3:00 a.m. when the baby's screaming and I'm wondering, *What's going on, God, and how do we deal with this?*

I believe God wants us to be engaged in these moments with our children, and all of the moments in between. I often hear talk in our circles about "God moments," times when something particularly amazing happens and we know God is involved. While I've experienced plenty of those and am so thankful for those times, I believe every minute we're drawing breath is really a "God moment." God is showing up in every moment and revealing something about Himself to us if we just have eyes to see it and ears to hear it, and most importantly a heart to receive it. I hope this book is your reminder of that today, right now.

Steven Curtis Chapman

God moments

Shaoey, Stevey Joy,
Steven, and Maria

spins and sways

She spins and
she sways

to whatever

song plays

without a care
in the world

Look

And I'm sitting here wearing

the weight of the world

on my shoulders

at me Daddy!

Bedtime rituals

At *bedtime*, when I walk into her room, I always

feel a little awed, like I'm walking on *sacred ground*.

Everything is so small and delicate, including

the *princess* who's climbing under the covers. Ever

since she was a baby, she's had me *mesmerized*.

One thing is for sure: her sweetly spoken

"Goodnight, Daddy" is the very best part of my day.

little-girl giggles

It's been a long day and
there's still work to do

She's pulling at me saying,
"Dad, I need you"

There's a ball at the castle
and I've been invited

and I need to practice my dancing
Oh please, Daddy, please

"*Kids:* they dance before they learn

there is anything that isn't music."

—William Stafford

She's standing in the kitchen in her princess

outfit, looking very much the part.

The *barefoot princess* twirls, her feet make tiny slaps

against the tile, and she *laughs* as her skirt

billows and falls. This is her favorite afternoon activity,

and you're her *number one fan.*

her dad's
favorite girl

It doesn't matter that her *crown* is lopsided

or that her dress has a chocolate milk stain.

It *doesn't matter* that the post office closes in an

hour; the tax forms can wait a few more minutes.

All that matters is that *right now*—in a moment

that will *last* in her heart forever—she is

her dad's favorite girl, the *center of his world.*

So I will dance with Cinderella

while she is here in my arms

'cause I know something
the prince never knew

Oh I will dance with Cinderella

I don't want to miss even one song

'cause all too soon the clock
will strike midnight

and she'll be gone

teach me
Daddy!

Sometimes the *best memories* aren't planned—

a skip in the *rain*

a *kiss* to heal teddy's torn paw

a hug *"just because."*

These spontaneous moments make

a permanent *place in our hearts.*

moments together

I attended my first Christian concert years ago at Samford University in Birmingham, and that was when I first saw Steven Curtis Chapman. Here was this very young, very energetic singer-songwriter that blew me away. Since then, he has continued to impress me with his ability to evolve and stay relevant not just in the sound of his music but in the message.

As his ministry expanded to include Shaohannah's Hope and his three personal international adoptions, he really did become my hero. He and Mary Beth became an inspiration to my wife and me as we adopted our two children. We adopted our son, Eli, domestically, and the three of us traveled to China to adopt our youngest, Naomi, when Eli was just three years old. We are so very thankful for all that Steven continues to do to make people more aware of the process of adoption.

Obviously, I have been a big fan of Steven's for years now, so I was thrilled to find out that this year he would be performing at Night of Joy at Disney World. I have seen him perform many times over the years, and I love the fact that his sons are now performing with him. I always enjoy hearing new versions of his greatest hits, but that night at Disney World, he sang one new song that absolutely knocked my knees out from under me.

He told a story about getting his youngest kids ready for bed, and then he sang "Cinderella" from his new project. As manly as we guys try to be most of time, I could not stop the tears from streaming down my face. My son and daughter are five and four years old, so I know the preschool years well, and I know what bath time, story time, and bedtime prayers are like. I, too, tend to rush through these daily rituals just to get to something that seems so much more important at the time.

"Cinderella" reminded me that nothing is more important in my life than my two angels. Right now is an incredibly important time in their lives, and nothing I do matters quite as much as being their dad. (And maybe the reason behind some of my tears was that I could so easily visualize my daughter dressed as Cinderella, just as the song describes.)

Because of that song, because of that moment as a fan in the crowd, I made time this morning just for my kids. They love to throw the football with me. They love it when I teach them how to hold the ball, stand, aim, and throw it in a perfect spiral. They love to try and catch my throws. They just love the chance to hang out and play with dad, since I tend to work a little too much, a little too often. I was three hours late for work today because of this planned time, and it was worth every minute of extra work I may have to do to make up for it.

I'm grateful for another wonderful song from one of my favorite artists, and for the way this song touched my life—as well as the lives of my kids.

Jeff Cruz
Altamonte Springs, Florida

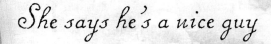

She says he's a nice guy

and I'd be impressed

She wants to know if I
approve of the dress

Caleb Chapman and Julia
headed to the prom.

She says, "Dad, the prom
is just one week away

and I need to practice my dancing

Oh please, Daddy, please"

Do you like my dress, Daddy?

Dance with me...

Wait a minute—*suddenly* she looks so *grown up*. Is she wearing makeup? And are those her mother's shoes? Just how *tall* is she, anyway?

It seems like five minutes ago she was just getting *her first haircut*. Now she's asking for her first cell phone. It all went by so *fast*— she's a *young lady* now.

"It will be gone before you know it. The fingerprints on the wall appear higher and higher. Then suddenly they disappear..."

—Dorothy Evslin

He'll always...

Steven and
Emily Chapman,
Emily at age 13 and then age 20.

I remember several years ago hearing a good friend say that he made a *commitment* to try to make sure his voice was the last one his daughter heard *every* night before she fell asleep. That sounded like great *wisdom*, so, from that night on, whenever it was physically possible, I would climb the stairs to her bedroom, tuck Emily in —*Queen Tuck*, as I called her—pray with her, and let the last thing she heard before she fell asleep be the voice of her dad saying, "*Goodnight, Em*. I love you." Those little moments are priceless to us now. —*Stu*

be here for me...

The first time I heard the song "Cinderella," I was listening to a radio station online during GMA week. I remember laughing when I heard the introduction to the song, a story about bath time with Mr. Chapman's little girls. When he began singing a beautiful acoustic version of "Cinderella," a wave of memories flooded my mind.

I think this song is a wonderful reminder not only for parents but also for children. Sometimes, we teenagers need to slow down and take the time to remember that being a child will not last forever, that our quality time with Mom and Dad will soon be spent. At this point in my life, it's almost time for me to start my own "great adventure" and leave home to go off to college with huge dreams to impact the world in some way that is still unknown. I can't listen to "Cinderella" without remembering special memories from when I was a young child and wishing that time hadn't passed so quickly.

I truly hope that "Cinderella" will bring back those memories for everyone who hears it, parents and kids alike. Cherishing memories can help us stay close to our parents, no matter where our dreams take us. Nothing can break the bond between parent and child, and memories can only strengthen that unbreakable bond.

Brandy Hensley
Corpus Christi, Texas

moments

My hero

"I'm *here* whenever you need me."

"*Please call* when you get there…"

"Don't be scared—I'm just down the hall."

"Being your dad is one of the absolute *greatest joys*."

"You're *so important* to me."

"You'll always be *my little girl*."

"Thanks for always *being there*, Dad."

"You don't need to worry,"

(but I love it that you do).

"*Thank you* for always being ready to listen."

"I really do appreciate *everything* you do for me."

"Dad, you'll always be *my hero*…"

My little girl

I will dance

So I will dance with Cinderella

while she is here in my arms

'cause I know something
the prince never knew

don't want to miss a

Oh I will dance with Cinderella

I don't want to miss even one song

'cause all too soon the clock
will strike midnight

and she'll be gone

basketball shoes and
little girl bracelets

it's the little things

Funny how things that used to annoy,

now seem *adorable*...

Strawberry shampoo in the bathroom,

basketball shoes in the middle of the doorway,

bracelets left on the coffee table.

These *little things* make me hope the bathroom

counter is always *cluttered*, the refrigerator door

always covered with schedules, and the

room *down the hall* always (a little) messy.

Okay, so sometimes I give my *dad* a hard time

for always being under the hood of my car

or freaking out about the *smallest* little things.

But *the truth is*, I love the way he jumps to

protect me. I know that's his way of making me

feel *loved and safe*. Still, it's hard not to laugh

at how his jaw gets so tense *every time*

I bring my boyfriend over to the house.

loved

" Watching your *daughter* being collected by her date feels like handing over a million-dollar Stradivarius to a gorilla. "

—Jim Bishop

My little girl…

She came home today

with a ring on her hand

just glowing and telling us

all they had planned

…all grown up

dance with me Daddy

She says, "Dad, the wedding's
still six months away

But I need to practice my dancing

Oh please, Daddy, please"

I knew this day was coming. I *heard* it in their

voices and the way they hinted toward the future.

And still it *caught me by surprise.* I'm

confident in them; I know this is a *wonderful* day,

and I really am happy. But there's this tiny little

tug in my heart, and part of me is only thinking

about how much *I'm going to miss her.*

My Cinderella

I have a Cinderella in my family...

And by the time this book is in your hands, she will be a Baylor University graduate. Her name is Emily, and she is all grown up. Wasn't it yesterday that she was spinning and swaying through childhood without a care in the world? It seems like a split second has gone by, and now she has spun and swayed herself into being a beautiful woman of God whom her father and mother are so proud of!

I remember my tears on Emily's first day of kindergarten—and suddenly she had twirled her way right through the knee-scraping elementary-school years. Believing that the agonizing and awkward middle-school years would never end, I was surprised that, in a blink of an eye, Emily was dancing herself right on through high school with all of the heartbreaks and amazing memories that come with those teenage years. And then, as if waking from a dream, I opened my eyes one day to find myself decorating a college dorm room in Texas.

Right before my eyes Cinderella was dancing herself into her own life. She would never dance herself out of our hearts, but somehow I knew, as Steven, Caleb, Emily, and I stood holding hands outside of her dormitory to say our good-bye prayers and give our parting hugs and kisses, that life would never be the same. Emily was indeed a grown princess ready to take on the world and become all that God had long intended her to be.

Knowing that our good and loving heavenly Father would be with Emily each moment of her life didn't make the ride home any easier for me. My tears flowed from Waco, Texas, all the way to Franklin, Tennessee. I guess that's just what we moms do....

Now, as I think about Shaohannah, Stevey Joy, and Maria, and all the challenges that come with raising these three little ones, one word keeps me going: *Emily*. The years go by in a heartbeat—and I pray you remember that! On those days when you're ready to give up because you're just plain tired and in those moments when you're absolutely out of patience or even questioning your parenting abilities, remember that it won't be long before you'll be watching your own princesses twirl right through your life and into lives of their own.

Because of Christ,

Mary Beth Chapman

Emily Chapman

fairy wings and pretend

So I will dance with Cinderella

while she is here in my arms

'cause I know something
the prince never knew

Oh I will dance with Cinderella

I don't want to miss even one song

'cause all too soon the clock
will strike midnight

and she'll be gone

No matter *how much* we might want

to slow time down and keep our

kids little, *change* is headed our way.

From a balloon that proclaims, "It's a Girl!"

to a fountain of *caps and gowns*

to "You may now kiss the bride."

Seize every opportunity to . . .

"Give your entire attention to what God is doing *right now*."

—Matthew 6:34

She spins and she sways
to whatever song plays

without a care in the world

And I'm sitting here wearing
the weight of the world on my shoulders

It's been a long day
and there's still work to do

She's pulling at me saying,
"Dad, I need you

there's a ball at the castle and
I've been invited

and I need to practice my dancing

Oh please, Daddy, please"

So I will dance with Cinderella

while she is here in my arms

'cause I know something the prince never knew

Oh I will dance with Cinderella

I don't want to miss even one song

'cause all too soon the clock will

strike midnight

and she'll be gone

not a care in the world

she says

She says he's a nice guy

and I'd be impressed

She wants to know if I approve of the dress

She says, "Dad, the prom

is just one week away

and I need to practice my dancing

Oh please, Daddy, please"

Oh I will dance with Cinderella

while she is here in my arms

he's a nice guy

'cause I know something the
                prince never knew

Oh I will dance with Cinderella

I don't want to miss even one song

        'cause all too soon the clock
            will strike midnight

and she'll be gone

She came home today
with a ring on her hand

just glowing and telling us
all they had planned

She says, "Dad, the wedding's still
six months away

But I need to practice my dancing
Oh please, Daddy, please"

So I will dance with Cinderella

while she is here in my arms

'cause I know something the prince never knew

Oh I will dance with Cinderella

I don't want to miss even one song

'cause all too soon the clock will strike midnight

and she'll be gone

dance with me, Daddy

In Steven Curtis Chapman's twenty-year career,

he has won five Grammys and an American

Music Award, achieved more number-ones and

more Dove Award nods than any other contemporary

Christian artist, and sold more than 10 million records.

Awards and album sales aside, Steven is possibly best

known for writing songs that have moved, inspired,

and encouraged a generation. He and his wife,

Mary Beth, have six children, Emily, Caleb, Will

Franklin, with their adopted daughters, Shaohannah,

Stevey Joy, and Maria. Shortly after adopting

their first daughter, Steven and Mary Beth established

Shaohannah's Hope, a foundation that assists families

hoping to adopt with information and

financial grants. Find out more

at ShaohannahsHope.org.

"Cinderella" graces Steven's latest album, *This Moment*, now available from Sparrow Records. For more information visit StevenCurtisChapman.com.